Feminism
Nick Monks

Bluebell Publishing

Title Page

Published by Bluebell Publishing- December 2019

Printed by Lulu
www.lulu.com

ISBN: 978-0-9955203-9-4

By the same author

Poetry

By the Canal (Masque Publishing)
Winter Trees
Cities Like Jerusalem
Homes
Narratives
Gardening
The Love Songs of James Dyer
Greek Olympian Myth
Imaginary Friends
Snow
England's of the Mind
Footprints (The Disparate)
Charlemagne's Rivers
American Realist Painters

Short Stories

Aegean Islands

Plays

Le Conquet (The Refugees)

For Amanda, Karl, Saskia

"Your body is for you, your writing is for you, your mind is for you, use it"- Helene Cixous

PREFACE

The first conflictual model of society is generally credited to the Russian renaissance thinkers. Whom Marx read.

Societies still have a long way to go to embrace- plurality/ diversity/ difference/. As personally one of the many who don't fit in. Many more people are in this category than would be apparent or guessed at.

I welcome anything that challenges the legitimacy of state. The models of civil society. Metaphysics and my place in. Most people view dialectical materialism relating to workers controlling society as surpassed. But the dialectics of conflictual have increased with feminism/ ethnic rights/ civil rights/LGTBI+

Some of the poems contain little lyrical quality. And are poems in the sense that line breaks are included. There primary role is to convey information.

Feminism as one strand of a rich vein of critical thinking in post modernism is valuable and needed. I hope the following poems will provide a brief informed structure and sketchy overview. That will be beneficial to the reader and stimulate further enquiry.

Contents

Feminism

Charlie

She turned up at tutorials with type written essays
And talked about her sore bum from the jogging excursion

She bought a bottle of fizzy Pomagne when I got appendicitis
Then she blanked me after the strategic gossip
While I got drunk and escaped into sport
She embraced English the English nasty feminism
Born in English social science and humanities departments

She got a 2:1 BA honours Phil
I fell into poverty and legal problems.

Two Days in the Life of Chloe

She left her three children with her mum
who owns a B and B in Blackpool
polished her nails blue and green
smeared lipstick on her face
wore a negligee under a baggy jumper
on the street corner
with two Irish drunks/alcoholics
she smokes cigars from the offy
the children of the revolution
go to the canal. And she chats to Keith
who's 32 and out fishing with his grandchildren
they borrow a car and drive to a day centre
where Emily and Jan colour in paintings
after drawing in the dot to dots
an enterprise to make and sell birthday cards
to keep the DWP happy.

And its only 2.50 pm

they go out back to the canal
where Josh is trying to shoot crows with a 2.2 air rifle
then five of them head back to her two up two down
where they burn josh sticks
and drink honeyed tea
she rings her mother in Blackpool-
to enquire about her three kids
they play Black Sabbath songs on the CD player
while the neighbours next door are having a domestic
involving shouting at each other

then she goes to sleep at Dianne's house
after a change of outfit and a phone call to Selima
tomorrow the pregnancy test will be positive.

Next Day 9.30 am

she cleans the house from top to bottom
for lunch has a pizza delivered
three of them smoke hashish
before dancing in a circle to Oasis and Marvin Gaye
they sit in the sun on the bench in the back yard
cycle to Claire's
who's binging on biscuits and sweets
she's got a dental appointment at 3pm
and sits in the waiting room giggling with Claire and Jess.

they buy a camera on the way home
let the pet rabbit out of the cage to wander
the wooden lounge floor
she fans her face with a Spanish fan bought at a car boot
they smoke more hashish, then at a loss what to do
play cards- gambling music cd's, then strip poker
without going all the way.

Its 7.10 pm

Fiona

1

She stood close to the mirror
smeared lipstick all over her face
then presented herself

she batted eyelids against my skin
on a cold Octobers day we said goodbye

i caught the flight to Buenos Aires
and never found my way back.

2

I came back from the flight to Havana
went to your flat, but you weren't there
i sat on the doorstep, after such a long journey
and reared out of control, like a falling star
to find its rest in the sea.

3

In this room, the rain on the window
at two am. I pick up a crayon
sketch the way back to you
in deductive logical equations.

when I was finished I went to the pub
got drunk and forgot about you
as I didn't have a gift from the gods

and you might not understand logic

i carried you in my heart and that is all
like an eternal secret wave polished pebble.

4

His dead body fell like a star
carried on the dark tide
his corpse wave lashed

the stars must know so much
not to blush, to keep their cool
the ocean hurts my skin
it was just a poem, Just caprice

as I hear you knock on the door
my pulse in turmoil once more.

Sojourner Truth (Isabella Belt Baumfree)
1797 to 26th November 1883

Born into slavery. In New York Swartekill, Ulster, but escaped with her infant daughter- to freedom in 1826. Abolitionist and women's rights activist. Spoke low Dutch. Known as Isabella. Couldn't read or write. Her parents where James and Betsey. The property of Colonel Johannes Hardenbergh.

She wanders the docks of Union City
A woman free by political activism
The Hudson a grey artery sash of water

In towns and cities
She delivers speeches to crowds of many-
Standing below the soap box intent avid-
On Sojourners words

She is passionate
Just, fair, RIGHT in her views

A free liberated woman
Freed in her quest for equal ethnic rights
Thus in the 19th C she has a referent subject self

She lives above the ruins of Chicago's abattoir
The breadline factories of the early 20th C
Above the pointless 1st and 2nd world wars
Above McCarthy's un American activities committee
Above poverty
Above the impoverished farm laborers

She is a princess in Guinevere s royal courts
A diminutive black woman in 1840

She is an am/ centuries ahead of her time

I buy a penny photograph of her
Return to my master's estate.

I am Nat Turner
Property of Samuel Turner of
Southampton county Virginia
I will lead 70 men in an armed revolt
And be hanged
As a reaction new laws will be passed to "control" blacks

My heir will be Martin Luther King
His heir will be Alice Walker
Her heir Austin Channing Brown

She had five children. Owned as a slave four times.
Travelled east coast and mid- west. Itinerant preacher of human
rights. Speaking forcibly for the abolition of slavery/women's
rights and suffrage/the rights of freedmen/ prison reform/
temperance/termination of capital punishment

Her biography was written by friend. *Narrative of Sojourner
Truth, A Northern Slave,* written by Olive Gilbert in 1850

Truth supported herself by selling portraits captioned:
"I sell the Shadow to support the Substance"

Famous speech given at Ohio Women's Rights Convention 1851
on racial inequalities- *"A'int i a Woman."*

Met Abraham Lincoln in 1864

During the civil war: She recruited black troops for the union
army. Tried to get land grants- unsuccessfully for former slaves

The pilgrim fathers had landed first
Now Sojourner wanders the east coast and mid- west

A vision is valuable, like water or air or wheat
So much so that her way is still here in the year 3034.

Estrogen, Testosterone

They are opposites.
Contrasting chemicals- needing each other

Testosterone is from Mars.
Oestrogen is from Venus

The directed aggressive structural vim searching
The receiving feel good/ am
Testosterone- structure/ Estrogen- nurture

Needing each other desperately
Seeking each other even without being aware

Like scorpions sex each is dangerous
Yet somehow the connection is made

Estrogen- women need just the right amount
Produced in larger amounts by women from the ovaries
And in smaller amounts via a gland above the kidneys
Permeates all the body
Formula $c18h24o2$
Also permeates other endocrine and non endrocrine tissues
Fat, liver, adrenal, breast, neural tissues

Estrradial is found in most vertebrates also fish, crustacea, insects

Estrogen regulates the functions of the menstrual cycle
Also makes women feel great

Testosterone produced mainly in male testicles
To lesser amount in female ovaries
An androgen chemical
Formula c19 h28 02.
Important for bone mass, muscles, bodily hair
Levels of testosterone are usually five times higher
In adult males than females
It is a naturally occurring steroid

Interesting facts about testosterone:

Women in initial stages of a love relationship have more, men
less than normal. Men have more testosterone leading up to a
sporting event.

In old age replacing testosterone doesn't lead to youth, virility,
non- baldness, weight loss etc- It's not that simple

Hormones are secreted compounds
That alter certain receptive organs
Hormones cause other cells tissues and organs
To behave or function differently
When your natural hormones function properly
Healthy messages spread throughout your body
To create proper development and health

Allows men to blank things and step out
Both polarities seek each other
Like salmon the Alaskan river- they were born in

The most fundamental difference between sexes is that of
chemicals
A difference that marks metaphysics and all endeavour

Estrogen versus testosterone
Testosterone versus estrogen

Estrogen affects every part of the body from head to toe
Affects mental health, physical health, emotional health, sexual
health

More active you are or stressed or ill, more estrogen you'll need
and produce, need less in sleep

HTR hormone replacement therapy

Common menopause symptoms such as hot flushes, brain fog,
Anxiety can begin in the brain. As a result of low or no estrogen.

Genetic Code

The difference between the sexes
Is the birth of all metaphysics

Males have one y chromosome and one x chromosome
Women have two x chromosomes

The female DNA has an x chromosome
The male a y chromosome

The y chromosome is one of the fastest
Evolving parts of human genome
200 y linked genes have so far been identified
Contains the SRY gene passed only from father to son
Humans 30% difference from chimpanzee
All y linked genes
Expressed as hemizygous present on only one chromosome.

The Subject

It has been argued
By some third wave feminists
That women don't have a
Self- referential subject/self
Because of patriarchy
And can only live through-
Or as an adjunct to men
Or by having children.

The First Wave/ Second Wave/ Third Wave

1st

The campaign for birth control, choice, suffrage- early 20th C.

2nd

For equal rights in pay. Also- equal rights in law. More metaphysical. Addresses sexuality. Past injustice. Roles of the genders- 1960'S To 70's.

3rd

Recognizes that there are many different types of women and that second wave- while progress was made, was biased towards white middle-class women. Embraces plurality, often overlaps with schools of thought in the post- modernist cannon- Current present epoch.

The Celtic Cross

The horizontal is for woman receiving
The vertical for upright man
Women like Danu or Rhiannon
Men like Pwyll or Lugh

Men like Derrida and Francois Lyotard
Women like Arundhati Roy, Helene Cixous and Luce Irigaray

The snow on the Brecon Beacons
A man and a woman meet
Leaving the valley coal town below
The wind in their hair as they carousel on the summit

Christian/Celtic symbol from the 9th through to 12th Century
Particularly in regions evangelized by Irish missionaries

There under the graveyard elms
Is a millstone grit cross
With a circle/nimbus on the upright vertical

The inscription reads "Here lies Rhiannon- Dark black haired
Celtic goddess, mistress of the Lake Fells, the Snowdonia, the
Brecon Beacons, the Salisbury Plain

And all the rivers and slopes of trees therein
She is our divine goddess ancestor

Mother of the Sussex Downs. Princess of the New Forest
A dancer in the slums of east end Victorian London."

Based on- John Irving- The World According to Garp

You carried on in a masculine way
Holding down a job in journalism
Financing a family of five
Feeling as though you were flying through the air
In a euphoric dream

Life got worse and worse
But you carried on, a bleak helpless despair increasingly engulfing
Your role job is as material provider to the family unit
Bravely holding to your last citadel as material provider
Until that too was taken away by cancer

You looked into Fiona's eyes
They were deliciously black fulfilling eyes, framed by natural
Blond hair. Dandelion blue eyes like Monet's waterlilies water.
Exploding in a northern lake like a fallen crashing star

She said be a writer- so you did
She said earn money- so you did
She said dream- so you did
She said let's have children- so you did- three
She said let's go on safari in Kenya
Cross the Atlantic by sail- boat- so you did.

You are the only man in a commune of feminists.
You tell yourself your privileged.- But your- not

Two of the women cut out their tongues as a protest

One is a stripper who thinks about the libido and sexuality
One is into black women activism
One is a theorist charting Hollywood starlet's bleak prospects
Cast off before they have learnt to use the beauty that is then
lost
One is a liberal theorist
One a narrative novelist on queer theory
One a poet and playwright writing on inequality

You renounced everything
And lived in a no sexually world

All penetration is rape/ women are not objects
Women have no subject except through men

No shoes walking barefoot along black streets
A mind of black psychosis
No sex, no libido, no desire
Cut off at the root of your mind
No colours, no light, no blister of connection

So now you are a feminist (but your also very ill)

A martyr who surgically removed your own sexuality
From your mind- as an experiment,
Leaving a deformed grotesque black angel

The logical map was faulty

Then you embraced affectivity theory and became spirited and
friendly
Chatting to shop keepers and attending writer's groups
I guess the roles we play as actors are subjective

Us passengers at times in an enchanted playground city.

Sappho

Lived on the Aegean island of Lesbos
Her persona much played upon by modern artists
Wrote beautiful poetry of love
And the ancient Greek politic
Perhaps the earliest written word feminist
Had three brothers
Parents wealthy but not named
Exiled to Sicily around 600 BC
Most of her poems are lost
Renowned in academic circles
Best known as symbol for same sex desire
Particularly female/ female
Most of her poetry lyric love poetry.

She stands on a cliff and asks of the waves divinity
The Aegean a mix of blues and inviting
Her hair whipped on this frontier promontory
Dressed in a blue silk dress
She dared to dive, such was her divinity she flew.

Her mien at the frontier
Of a world tuning up violins and cellos
A dance. That the world may begin
And Sappho become the fragrant source
Of developing fables,
Around a fire in a forest in Bretagne- her lineage continues
As Bretons narrate stories.

Julia Kristeva

Born in Bulgaria, moved to France. Prominent in structuralist, post structuralist thought. Addresses semiotic, intertextuality, abjection

I love your recognition that even
Relative health and material abundance
Is bleak, abject, horrible
I like the picture of you on powers of horror best
Of which I've found many versions on google images

She is in Provence chatting at an outdoor table
Arrayed with glasses and cheese slices and olives

And from the abundant wholeness of the psyche
An inversion by Freud of Greek deities
As most new ideas are:
Eg Fichte's inversion of the Hegelian dialectic

I read about the book of Ruth and Peregrinus in Rome/ Thomas Paine /Sigmund Freud/Stendhal/Jean Guyon/ Bernard de Clairvaux

Will you be my lawfully wedded patient/ reader?
As you psychoanalyse for me, I prescribe for thee

Also published under her married name Julia Joyaux

She favours a subject always "in process" or "on trial"
Her work could be seen as a psychoanalytic,

Approach to post structuralist criticism

Studied under Mikhail Bakhtin and later Roland Bathes
Follows for the most part Lacan's model for psychosexual
Development. But adds more emphasis on the maternal and
feminine

For this reason more amenable to feminist psychoanalyst looking
For a less sexist and phallocentric model for the subject

In powers of horror. Details how the horrific forces- the subject
to choose. And become.

Philosophical models of the psyche focus on whether the psyche
is a concept

Even though the psychoanalytic approach is flawed
The psyche in which she thinks Freud made a major
Advance holds the diverse references together
Personally I disagree and think the psyche may not
Exist save as an academically formulated concept.

Helene Cixous 5th June 1937-
A Stone Falls Forever

I like the picture of a slim you on your "Love in the Letter Box"
best
In vivid coloured clothes.
With severe cut blonde hair

I am not ashamed of my attachment to you

If we met my world would be kaleidoscope quantum
So I don't want to meet you.
I just want you to destroy planet earth
From the divinity French republic with words
Alternatively save the earth in the spite of the them's

Your words are quantum love
Indefatigable: the wolf, the lamb/ stigmata/ mindfulness /roots/
Dreams/ death/ loss/ generations

Concerned with what it is to be a foreigner. Jewoman, born in
1937 in Oran Algeria. S-he
A hybrid city "full of neighbourhoods, of peoples, of languages"

I read your essays about your father in Morocco a doctor
Your room and a bird flying indoors
About the passion of Clarice Lispector- confronted with a
Cockroach in the book - "The Passion According to GH"
About posting a letter
About Leonardo Da Vinci- "painting death"

Helene Cixous measures the air in a room of writing endeavour
Calibrates the beatings of a butterfly's wings from the room
balcony

Don't bother with ideology Helene
The words rhythm themselves will guide you
Like the sea currents, stars water chemistry
Guide salmon, whales, penguins, sharks

Let us elope to Marrakech.
You could write your ideas
Me my poetry
We could muse on a robin on the garden holly bush
Write of the wind in the Atlas mountains
Walk hand in hand into the Sahara forever

The snow of the Atlas mountains.
Us two horses alone.
Galloping into the sand dunes.
Continuing into the vast blister of desert

Her "escaping text" language, make her work a joy to read

In "The Cry of the Medusa"
Cixous advocates women must write
To gain authority back from patriarchy
The term "White Ink" is often used
"Writing is for you, you are for you, your body is for you, take it"

We travel together over the deserts, forests, lakes
Of Avalon and to Atlantis
A woman more- large than the world.

Luce Irigaray

Born 1930 3rd May

Belgian born psychoanalyst, linguist, philosopher, cultural theorist, psycholinguist, feminist

Best known works "Speculum of the Other Woman" 1974
"This Sex Which is Not One" 1977

Says women traditionally associated with matter
And nature to the exclusion of the female subject position
Women can become subjects by assimilating to the male subject
A separate subject position for women does not exist

Subsequent texts provide critique and analysis of the exclusion of women from:
History of philosophy, psychoanalytic theory, structural linguistics

Shows that an aeons old trajectory
Is taking people away from the
Connection with self and nature

Argues in "Spectrum"
Women are treated like commodities
Drawing on Marx-
Have a use and exchange value

From academic isolation grew this connectedness of her theory

In- "In the Beginning She Was" demonstrates how:
From the beginning western tradition represents an exile for humanity

The necessity of art as a mediation towards another culture
The limits of western logic
The sexuation of discourse
Transforming our instincts into shareable desires
Looks at pre- Socratic roots
Man elaborated a discourse of mastery
Constructed a world of his own
That grew away from life
And prevented perceiving the real as it is
Ostracized from some academic circles for her views
Currently teaches at Warwick University, Midlands UK.

Hannah Arendt
14th October 1906 to 4th December 1975

I like the picture of you with fawn bob of hair
"To reiffify the previous male bias in the history of human
thought"
You tread through the world of abstract thought
Like a Sorbonne philosopher
You have lived your whole life in the ecstasy the-
Brazen delicious beauty of abstract ideas.
Like Sibelius, like the Bewick swan, the dislodged snow from pine
Tops, the exact hue of the nights cloak, submits and bows to your
charge
The others are sassy, laugh prone, hysterically sane, materialistic,
disingenuous
I found your books on violence and revolutions refreshingly
accurate
And loved your book "Eichmann on trial"
Agreeing that evil is just boring and there's a lot of it everywhere
And when I move laterally tangentially to the side
Yes the world makes sense and MY past is not just a commodity
To ditch in the cognitive euphoria of the present
I love your analyses of spaces- the private, the public
Hope you build a city of women's ideas
I think of you every day, and am privileged to read you books

The beauty of abstract analytics
Expanding the idioms pointing out that though
Often forgotten America was born of a revolution
Expanding the idiom of violence-
Even poverty is i think is a form of violence

German born political theorist
Jewish, escaped the holocaust

Attempts to redress the male imbalance in the history of thought
Available the objective structures and characteristics of
Political-being-in- the-world
As a distinct mode of human experience

In Chatelet she walks an anonymous philosopher.
Hood on to the rain. Along Rue St- Martin.
Glances in a bookshop. Towards the gardens of Luxembourg.
Before returning to read Levi Strauss in the apartment home

"Modernity was a case of the mass loosing self to the totalitarian
bureaucracy"

Her works on diverse subjects: revolution, violence,
Nature of freedom, faculties of thought and judgment,
Totalitarianism

Hollywood film was made about her.

Judith Butler

An academic celebratory
Jewish, lesbian, anti- Semite

Her views of performativity empowers and frees

In New York urban cosmopolitan
A largesse intellectual in phenomenology
Good understanding of areas of thinking
And ontological epistemology

Effortlessly
Guiding
The errant through the philosophy
Of otherness
In fear and trembling
We see
We gauge
We measure
We live
We act

Never able to resolve
The angst of life, or otherness

Analytically adept
An anti- Zionism Jew

You could justifiably claim Brooklyn bridge from Hart Crane

Looked at sexual identity

Distinction sexual act and cultural gender-
Society ascribes to it, performativity or theatrical gender

Queer theory

The angels, prostitutes and policemen
And ex- cons inhabit the city sewers
Judith and I are by the Hudson
As the Clash sing London Calling and Blondie- Union City Blue
Across the water. Manhattan scrapers struts
Their accomplishments of the modern

Argues that Beauvoir and Irigaray assume a fixed female identity
But gender and bodies Butler argues are
Performative, and influenced by (me- finances, power relations,
judiciary etc) Butler- (class, ethnicity, sexuality etc)

Identity itself for Butler
Is an illusion retroactively created by our performance's

"Bodies agencies providing opportunities to subvert the law
against itself to radical, political ends"
"There is no existence that is not social"

I walk in the theatre and take my place
In Moliere's penned play
The finale is ruin. My tragedy. Then Judith in the crowd
Bequeaths a new script of freedoms that I write in
The social play of surfaces.

Emma Goldman

June 27^t 1869 to May 14th1940

Born in Kovno Russian empire
Present day Lithuania
Emigrated to America in 1885
Became a writer renowned lecturer
Attracting crowds of 1000's
On anarchism philosophy, women's rights, social issues
New York, New York
Theatre of becoming
The breath of the new
Emigrated to USA from Russia
Died in Canada at age of 70
Deported to Russia
Initially supported the
October revolution, then not
Lived in France, Britain, Germany
Thousands listened to her speeches
She and her partner anarchist writer Alexander Berkman
Planned to assassinate financier and industrialist Henry Clay Frick
As an act of propaganda of the deed
Frick survived the attempt in 1892
Berkman was sentenced to 22 years
She was imprisoned multiple times for inciting to riot
And distributing information on birth control
In 1906 she founded the anarchist journal "Mother Earth"
Advocated birth control as Margaret Sanger did
Tried to persuade men not to register for armed service in Great
War

You dancing, your wild child stillness

God damned anarchists
In and out of prison
As sure as I am James Dyer in 2035
That my vision is valid
You're a damsel of truth an indomitable
What brazen spirit

Vision more valuable than bacs credits of barristers and
Psychiatrists, than ATOS forms, Brexit negotiations, going abroad,
Restaurant goodbyes, public houses, supermarkets

Increase of interest in her from feminists in 1970's
Let us say you here so ahead of your time you are eternal.

Margaret Sanger

B Sep 4th 1879 in Corning New York to Sep 6th 1966 aged 86

American feminist
In the first wave
Born sept 17th 1879
In 1915 obscenity laws
Forced her to flee country
Arrested at least eight times during her career
Advocated birth control
Opened the first birth control clinic in America
Formed the Planned Parenthood Federation of America

Practicalities change and make life's feasible
Ahead of her time

Supported black community
Involved black ministers in contraception
For poor black communities
Fought for free speech on contraception
Which was banned in America
Helped by Emma Goldman
Nurse, writer, family planning,
Birth control activist, sex educator

In 1965 the supreme court division
Griswold v Connecticut made birth control legal for married
couples.

Florence Nightingale
12 May 1820 to 13 August 1910

Isn't generally regarded as a feminist
Statistician, founder of modern nursing, social reformer
Cared for soldiers in the Crimean war
Thus bringing in for the first time
The hospital environment and system of nascent health care

Nurse, nurse water please
The pain now bearable
Mutated into the evil monster of the NHS

A row of beds in Crimea,
Hundreds of men in wards
Being treated in a clean environment
Injured soldiers

Trained nurses to tend during the Crimean war
The lady with the lamp-
Making rounds of wounded
Soldiers in the night

In 1860 set up a nursing school at St Thomas's hospital
First secular nursing school in the world
She was an icon of Victorian culture

Nightingale pledge taken by new nurses
And the Nightingale medal is the highest International distinction
a nurse can receive

The night cool air. Wafting on the injured

43

Who await on beds under cool sheets
As nurses in uniforms tend the sick

The high buildings. Corridors in pale blue
The butterflie's wings tattered now in autumn.

Emily Davison

11th October 1872 to 8th June 1913

Threw herself under the kings George 5 horse-
Amner at the Epsom derby on June 4th 1913
Died from her injuries 4 days later
Arrested 9 times
Force fed 49 times while incarcerated
In the first wave in Britain
Feminists also put bombs in letterboxes
Damaged a building in Kew gardens
The authorities reacted with cat and mouse
Locking women up
Releasing them before their hunger strike killed them
And trying to prevent publicity
Emily Davison's act hit the front pages
Lloyd George denied women suffrage
Which was granted in the 1930's
Other prominent feminists of this time and era were Emmeline
Pankhurst, Millicent Garratt Fawcett, Sylvia Pankhurst (daughter
of Emmeline)

Her funeral on 14th June organized by
Women's Social and Political Union, WSPU
Tens of 1000's lined streets of London
Thousands of suffragettes accompanied the coffin

Buried in Morpeth church in Northumberland
Her headstone inscription reads "deeds not words"

A martyr for future generations
An antecedent worthy of our dreams

She stands with the respectable well- dressed onlookers
As the horses galloping come closer
And the prison stays. The disapproval. The harassment of their campaign
The knowledge that the suffragettes are right
Springs to one piano note. To a violin air
The violent lunge into the race tracks verdant lush green
The terrible thump of a shocked body

Gained a BA from London university
1st class honours degree Oxford University
Which was unusual for a woman at that time

Was appalled by the lack of opportunity for women
And the degrading lack of a woman's vote.

The Past, Matriarchal

It is possible that in some distant world
Women were whole
In the beginning, the inception, the start,
And we have destroyed the balance
Between dark and light
As we seek to force the world and people
To our will

Was there ever a woman centred past epoch?
Even if not that doesn't make it less valid

A world where woman was divine
And reverenced as the source and essence
A world before these things that be
The money, industry, technology that enrich our life- but was
there the divine female in the past

Lets say The Karen tribe in the forests of Burma grew rice in small
paddocks, hunted wild boar. Painted themselves red. Looked to
the elder chief to resolve disputes. Lived in huts of palm trees
The woman the sage and worshiped.

Mosuo tribe Tibet- children stay with mother, make business
decisions, walking marriages, woman walks to mans hut- don't
stay together, ownership of goods passed down matrilineal lines.

Nagovisi in New Guinea- Anthropologist Jill Nash reports- society
divided into two matrilineal moieties. Then divided into
matriclans. Women involved in ceremonies and leadership. Work

the land entitled to them. Marriage not institutionalized. If couple seen together. Sleep together. Man assists woman in her garden. Then for all intents and purposes. Seen as married.

The White Goddess

Somewhere before the Greek golden age
It is rumoured
The woman was the godhead
Before we journeyed far
Always wishing to return
Where are we going?
In the forests once covering Britannia
Are silicon conductors, fibre optics, stem cells
The considered Avalon
Robert Graves argued the worship of a goddess is
The most- pure form of religion
And the source of all good poetry.

Mary Wollstonecraft

27 April 1759 to 10 September 1797

English writer, philosopher and advocate of women's rights
Best known for "A Vindication of the Rights of Women" 1792

I envision you on a ship
Carrying like Keats
Your desires like a prayer
Yes I admire you
Love you even
As you are there, enlightened and politically aware
In the dark turrets of gothic castles
Archers and cannon soldiers are training their weapons
And in this dank Celtic gothic world
You shed light and clothes
And suffer from desire

You wrote "Mary or the Wrongs of Women" in 1792
The date today is 24/11/19 and 00:18 am and I am thinking of
you
One of her two daughters Mary Wollstonecraft Godwin
Wrote as Mary Shelley "Frankenstein"

"Vindication of the Rights of Women" response to Edmund
Burkes- "Reflections on the Revolution in France"
"Maria or the Wrongs of Women"- posited that women have
strong sexual desires
And degrading and immoral to pretend otherwise
This damned her in eyes of critics for the century to come
Worked on journal "Analytical Review" launched by Johnson in
1788

Unhappy for most of life
Believed in sensibility (then a derogatory term for women) more
than in rationality

Concerned for political rights for women and desire
And women's need for self/subject and emotional romance

In London with the deadline approaching for
The article in "Analytical Review"
A prophetess of the future
Writing perhaps out of need
For a secondary world to escape her woes
London- the office- the article for "Analytical Review"
Is apt and enlightening. Back to her – "A Room of One's Own."

Bible Feminism

There are as few as only forty- nine named women who speak in
the bible
While over 3000 named men

Ruth is an interesting and profound book
Profoundly articulating about strangers in Judaism
Integrating into the community
Mary Magdalen is very important in the gospels
Was present at the crucifixion
And first to see resurrected Jesus
Many scholars think she had a better understanding of the new
covenant than the male disciples
Salome asked for John the Baptist's head

18000 wandering the desert, will we ever be free

The bibles theology though is not anti- women
Talking of rejuvenation of the mind,
The fruits of work connected to the vine
Freedom by the redemption of the crucifixion
Faith and its strength

Ways the bible supports feminism:

God assigns dignity to all human beings
God assigns important work to all
Each contributes their unique strengths
Humans are sinful, but atoned by the crucifixion
God calls Christians to fight injustice

The spirit of Jesus can restore broken divided humans to unity
and wholeness

The C of E rejected women bishops in 2016.
The Catholic church rejects women Priests

Biblical teaching has empowered many women to succeed in this
epoch

By embracing Christianity blacks in America have taken the
Chalice and enacted inclusivity
Appropriated the white man's source.

Hinduism and Feminism

There are female gods
As well as male gods
The gods and goddesses
Are regaled as statues in Hindu Temples
And portrayed in the Vedas, the Upanishads, the Bhagavad Gita
The practitioner's project self onto the gods and goddesses
Meaning they can be personal for each individual
Much kinder to women than Christianity

Bryant goddess source divine
In other places women told to honour father then husband then
son
Some scholars think old texts have been corrupted
Points to the difference between the soul and the flesh
As the soul has no gender men and women are equal

Feminine power is revered in the form of goddesses
And the concept of Shakti
Both sexes equal in yogic power or enlightenment

Western material way of living
Hindu Sanatana Dharmic way

Many Hindu women make valued and worthwhile
Contribution to British and European societies

They seem more grounded and intellectual than
Their white Christian or secular counterparts.

Three Women

1

She works as a social worker
In an office
In an advisory capacity to 190 social workers
In the field of child- care
Is enthusiastic committed and resilient
Good at her job and has a positive
Effect on the outcomes of her social workers clients

2

She is manager of a Tesco express
Deals with:
Accounts, staffing, shelf displays
The job keeps her a calm approach
Making sure the store runs smoothly
And staff and customers are happy

Has two children which are looked after by her parents while she
is at work

3

She is a teacher of physics at a sixth form college
Did a Bse in physics at Loughborough
In a male dominated sector has good A level pass rates
Getting 90% of students A to C grade
Works and travels and climbs mountains for leisure

LTGBI+

In a way LGTBI+ are mimicking heterosexual society

Some allow children to choose their gender orientation
Regardless of biological fact

Many of LTGBI+ community active in feminism
Many are not

In a liberal society people-
Should be allowed however
To orientate themselves however they wish
Between concentrating adults
Romans 1 in the new testament criticizes non- heterosexuality

Most feminists are accepting of LGTBI+
Some of them are feminists
Other feminists believe in binary roles.

The Libido

Sexuality is Thanatos/Eros
It invokes
What the subject does with their sexuality
Determines the outcomes of their life
A woman should use her sexuality for her benefit

And In the idyll of Atlantis
A man tall. And a woman with raven hair
Stand by a silver lake
Each within each other. Cleaving
The stretching forest
Bordering an azure ocean shore.

Alice Walker

Her book "The Colour Purple" was beautiful
An advocate of equality of gender, race, creed
Charts the life's of people aiming for aspiration
Has regrettably elitist views on artists

In "Meridian"- a black girl becomes and
Throws off the shackles of segregation
Opening a future- we all yearn for

Meridian Hill student at a fictitious Saxon College
Involved in civil rights movement
Made pregnant by another white activist Truman Held

Impregnates her, they have on off relationship
She has an abortion
Become closer together
Truman becomes involved with a white woman
Lynn Rabinowitz who is also involved in civil rights struggle
Though perhaps for the wrong reasons

As time goes by Truman unsuccessfully tries to achieve
Personal and financial success
Meridian continues in activist politics

Alice Walker's daughter Rebecca Walker edited the book of
feminist essays "To Be Real."

Maya Angelou

Wrote three volumes of her autobiography
An actor
Poet
Traveller
Activist
"I Know Why the Caged Bird Sings" my favourite
Autobiographical about early life
Travelled and lived in Liberia, Africa
Before returning to America
Poems also very good
About amongst other things poverty and hope
Following on from the jazz age
Were blacks in segregated America
Found a voice through jazz
She led a full and aspirational life
"Were rats eat cats of the leopard type/
And Sunday lunch is grits and tripe"
Other poems "And Still I Rise"

Rhiannon
Welsh Goddess

Celtic mythology existed amongst the iron age Celts across
Britain, Ireland and into central Europe

It remained most prevalent in the areas not suppressed by the
Roman invasion. Such as Scotland, Wales, Ireland, Brittany,
South West England. Was eventually superseded by Christianity.
Rhiannon is Welsh in origin.

-

There is a piece of paper lying crunched inexplicably on the
kitchen floor. Amidst the debris of a ransacked, emptied bin bag.
James Dyer a tobacco addict teetotalling civil servant unravels the
pieces of paper on impulse. Discarded by an ancient dark,
sorrowful, wise, Celtic poet. The paper chronicles Rhiannon high
priestess/goddess of Briton and Gaul and Ireland, here lies the
testament

—

Rhiannon puts on her coat
Finds her shoes
Picks up her car keys
Gathers herself,
Walks out of the front door
Parks the car in Fulwood, Preston

A passerby, walking the dank neon
Streets of Preston, Fulwood.
Like Raphael Soyer- The Passerby- painting
A woman amidst diversions

The shoddy and divine
Petrol stations/takeaways/neon road signs

Coat collar turned up- hurrying along
Splatters of blue rain from a darkened unnoticed sky

There are 7 portraits of Rhiannon

Egon Schiele- Woman With Knees Drawn Up
Raphael Soyer- The Annunciation
Dante Gabriel Rossetti- Persephone
Sargent- Cashmere
Sargent- Rosina Ferrara
Da Vinci- Mona Lisa
Whistler- Girl in white

—

She is mist and heather pollen and red grouse's wings
She is cigarette butts and broken glass, glistening pavement
puddles
Disappearing over the moors summit in purple hooded shawl

Artemis

Artemis has a large case load
There's 45 more people to see that day
Then eight letters to write

She dreams of the Caledonian forests
Nestled around the Cairngorms massif

She is the team leader of 40 social workers
Dealing in children and families
Covering 400 client families

A kid is screaming in the waiting room
I hear terrible things happened to that kid

Artemis bestows divine gifts on client women
There are four social workers waiting to see her
She is dead beat- tired

A thousand arrows to kill deer or wild boar
A cheerful smile at 6 pm

Artemis is a social worker in family child-care
Enthusiastic, ironic, sober, cheerful

Her files are written in five minutes
After each meeting- like the Eleusinian mysteries

"Artemis never dreams she is too tired"

The office has pale green walls
On her desk is a glass tray with baubles
The air conditioning keeping the offices at 19 degrees Celsius

The snow peaked mountain range of Olympus
The ice shards in the forest rivers
Nymphs surround her in a forest

She picks her two children up from school
And makes them tea
Helps them with their homework
Puts them to bed watches tv
Then goes to bed herself to wake for work tomorrow

As the traffic roars outside.
She is making a cup of coffee 3000 years old.

Karl Marx

Following on from the Russian renaissance thinkers
And Fichte's inversion of the Hegelian dialectic
Karl Marx and others in the internationals
Theorised in erudite volumes of philosophy, history, economics,
sociology
Posited dialectical materialism as increasing-
Conflicts in capitalism lead to a workers socialist state
That the world could be seen in terms of conflict of interest
Thus paving the way for feminism/ ethnic rights/ civil rights
movements/ difference/sexual difference/plurality

Marxist feminism looks at way women are oppressed by
Economic capitalism and the ownership of private property.

Madam Bovary- Flaubert

Gustav Flaubert's debut novel
Considered his masterpiece
The modern narrative- James Wood (British critic)
Our human condition. Faced with a repressive
Time and epoch

She tried to achieve meaningful life
Through emotions
Her situation likened to millions of people in 2052
Only to be killed by
French repressive patriarchy
She was married to a doctor
Called Emma Bovary
Lived beyond her means

Had an illicit affair to try and rejuvenate her subjugated life
Lost her marriage and died by self- poisoning horribly
Her desire mirrored in the post- modern human condition

Similar to- The Deep Blue Sea by Rattigan

The pit falls of desire and even aspiration apply to
Men too. Though many Hollywood films concentrate on a
heroine.

Terence Rattigan- Deep Blue Sea

Heroine leaves husband a judge
To live in a flat
With an airplane tester pilot
Tries to commit suicide
Discovery of Hester Collyer collapsed
Treated by a doctor who has been struck off

In the final scene
Her elope airplane pilot leaves her
Then Hester making and eating scrambled eggs. And crying

Play takes place over one day
Shows thwarted aspiration and desire
As incumbent in the post- modern condition

Both Madam Bovary and The Deep Blue Sea similar
Need for circumspection and self- control in desire
Which is natural and common to all humanity.

Hollywood

The seedy dank repressive town
Her yearning and aspirational
Becoming the heroine/ hero
Transformative light/transformative being

Her rejected. The dream ignited with cold fervour.

The fire sweeping through the flat
The axe wielding clown
The love affair over
From an opulent house/farm
To a seedy downtown single room
The burgeoning threads of dream intact in squalor

The car won't start
As a green alien approaches
Which pulls off the car roof
The car starts. But it's on fire now
He closes his eyes. Waits to be devoured
Then it rains heavily
The alien (badly burnt) falls away as the car accelerates
He drives away to a new life.
Through the smashed fence
A new world. A new self
Stopping at a road direction sign
Hesitating and choosing Colchester over Norwich.

Three Women

Diane Waddington

She wakes at 7am in New York
Drives the children to the day care
She then drives to the solicitor's offices
She has two deals to close that day
Is at the files at 8.30am to prepare
At 4pm after a day with multiple hitches and problems
The two deals are contract signed
And she goes to pick up her children.

Sheryl

Lives in Paris in Montreuil
Works as the manager of a branch travel agency.
Directs the staff.
Makes decisions on travel packages
Evaluates holiday destinations and hotels and tours
Swapping roles with other senior staff

On Saturday evening sits in a café in Chatelet.

Jess

Wakes up in Warrington
Has four children

Works part time as a cleaner
In a train station- 6am to 8am
Four days a week
Lives in a two bedroomed flat
In a new housing estate
Is desperately short of money and claims working tax credits.

Echo

Has society found redemption- no
Have these women found redemption- no!

But still over the September farm fields
The poppies and buttercup shimmer
In cascading colour.
The distant hills complete the moment and moments
Monet's haystacks bequeathed in decked colour
As us passengers in an exotic spellbound play
Rain on the grey dawn tarmac road.

Ophelia

"She'd prophesize between her cigarettes"- Natalie Marchant from the song- Ophelia

Her betrothed Hamlet
Forever the oedipal prince
She wandering like Marie Antoinette
Around the deserted Canary Warf pale green corridors
She gables and laughs with her royal court
She is every woman
As gabbled as her fiancé Hamlet the eternal prince in waiting
Who jumps in a grave holds up a skull
And says "Alas poor Yorick I knew him well"
Giggling in the embroidery room
Plotting an architecture of love
Her mad fiancé out in the forest
Intent on ridiculous folly
"Very like a whale" say his courtiers to Hamlets comments about a cloud
Her a child of the futile. Ardent and prophesising.
Her the nascent possibility's of womanhood.

Ruth

A stranger and poor
Listens to the advice of Naomi
An older woman
Naomi is rewarded by unfailing loyalty
In Ruth courage and ingenuity triumph over misfortune
Celebrates the family
And their way continues over generations
Becomes great grandmother of Israel's great king David

Even Ruth a foreigner from the despised Moabites
Could move gods plan towards fulfilment
Universal theme.
In the promised land
Married into the Jewish lineage
The eternal stranger- "for you were a stranger once"
A woman who prevailed by faith.

Some Feminists

Alejandra Pizarnic/ Halina Poswiatowska/ Gloria Gervitz/ Sylvia Plath/Jane Birkin/ Evita/Frida Kahlo/Tracey Smith/Mercedes Roffe/ Maria Baranda/ Mercedes/ Allyssa Monks/Elizabeth Robinson/ Roselle Angwin/ Carrie Etter/ George Eliot/Muriel Rukeyser/Clarence Lispector/ Marianne Faithful/ Margaret Atwood/ Forough Farrokhzad/ Elsa Cross/ Rosalia de Castro/Anne Carson/PJ Harvey/Debbie Harry/ Patti Smith/ Susanne Howe/ Fanny Howe/Veronika Volkow/Hanne Bramness/ Cecilia Vicuna/Emily Bronte/ Ann Bronte/ Charlotte Bronte/ Jane Austin/ Anna Akhmatova/ Maria Tsvetaeva/

Statement of Human Rights UN- found poem

Universal Declaration of Human Rights
Preamble
Whereas recognition of the inherent dignity and of the equal
and inalienable rights of all members of the human family is
the foundation of freedom, justice and peace in the world,
Whereas disregard and contempt for human rights have
resulted in barbarous acts which have outraged the
conscience of mankind, and the advent of a world in which
human beings shall enjoy freedom of speech and belief and
freedom from fear and want has been proclaimed as the
highest aspiration of the common people,

Whereas it is essential, if man is not to be compelled to
have recourse, as a last resort, to rebellion against tyranny
and oppression, that human rights should be protected by
the rule of law, Whereas it is essential to promote the
development of friendly relations between nations,

Whereas the peoples of the United Nations have in the
Charter reaffirmed their faith in fundamental human rights,
in the dignity and worth of the human person and in the
equal rights of men and women and have determined to
promote social progress and better standards of life in larger
freedom,

Whereas Member States have pledged themselves to
achieve, in cooperation with the United Nations, the
promotion of universal respect for and observance of human
rights and fundamental freedoms, Whereas a common
understanding of these rights and freedoms is of the
greatest importance for the full realization of this pledge,

Now, therefore, The General Assembly, proclaims this Universal Declaration of Human Rights as a common standard of achievement for all peoples and all nations to the end that every individual and every organ of society, keeping this Declaration constantly in mind, shall strive by teaching and education to promote respect for these rights and freedoms and by progressive measures, national and international, to secure their universal and effective recognition and observance, both among the peoples of member States themselves and among the peoples of territories under their jurisdiction.

Article I

All human beings are born free and equal in dignity and rights. They are endowed with reason and conscience and should act towards one another in a spirit of brotherhood.

Article 2

Everyone is entitled to all the rights and freedoms set forth in this Declaration, without distinction of any kind, such as race, colour, sex, language, religion, political or other opinion, national or social origin, property, birth or other status.

Furthermore, no distinction shall be made on the basis of the political, jurisdictional or international status of the country or territory to which a person belongs, whether it be independent, trust, non-self-governing or under any other limitation of sovereignty.

Article 3

Everyone has the right to life, liberty and security of person.

……… note continues